THE LIBERTY STYLE

Mahogany music cabinet, probably designed by Leonard Wyburd, made in Liberty's workshops, c. 1897.

THE LIBERTY STYLE

ALL COLOUR PAPERBACK

Introduction by

VICTOR ARWAS

RIZZOLI
NEW YORK

ACKNOWLEDGEMENTS
I should like to thank Haslam & Whiteway for allowing us to photograph the
cabinet in Plate 8, A. Papadakis for furniture photographed for plates 1-7,
the Victoria and Albert Museum for permission to reproduce works in
their possession (plates 13 and 47) and Bowes Museum, Barnard Castle
(frontispiece). I am particularly grateful to Liberty & Co. Ltd. and the
Victoria Library for allowing us to photograph from their 'Dress and
Decoration' catalogue (plates 9-12) and for providing transparencies of
fabrics (plates 14-16). All other items are from Editions Graphiques Gallery,
London.

First published in the United States of America in 1979 by
RIZZOLI INTERNATIONAL PUBLICATIONS, INC.
    712 Fifth Avenue/New York 10019
Copyright © 1979 Academy Editions London

Library of Congress Catalog Card Number 78-66216
ISBN 0-8478-0208-6

Printed and bound in Hong Kong

The names of certain shops recur consistently in the history of the development of Art Nouveau. In Paris, S. Bing's L'Art Nouveau, which gave its name to the movement, and Meir-Graefe's La Maison Moderne were the two shops which commissioned, fostered, encouraged, retailed and publicised the style. In England, Liberty & Co. was the shop which brought an original contribution to Art Nouveau.

Arthur Lazenby Liberty was born on 13th August 1843 over his father's little draper's shop in Chesham, a market town in Buckinghamshire. His family later moved to Nottingham, where an uncle of his had a lace warehouse. The boy was sent to the town's University School, but his father's finances were too low to keep him in school, so the lad worked briefly in his uncle's lace warehouse, then as a clerk in a wine warehouse before being apprenticed at the age of sixteen to a draper in London. Liberty hated the work, but spent as much of his free time as possible visiting galleries and the theatre. The apprenticeship was curtailed after two years and the boy was free to move. He soon found employment at Farmer and Rogers' Great Shawl and Cloak Emporium in Regent Street, that supremely elegant shopping street designed by Nash in which butchers, greengrocers and public houses were not allowed.

Liberty joined Farmer and Rogers in 1862. This was also the year in which an International Exhibition was held in Kensington, in which the Pre-Raphaelites exhibited their paintings; the Morris, Marshall and Faulkner Company first exhibited their wares, designed by Rossetti, Philip Webb, William Morris and Burne-Jones; and a representative collection of arts and crafts from Japan was on view. Farmer and Rogers bought the bulk of the Japanese exhibits after the exhibition, and opened an oriental warehouse as an extension of their store. Liberty was chosen as one of its two employees: two years later he became its manager.

The vogue for blue and white porcelain and for beautiful, soft, oriental fabrics, brought all the leading artists to the Emporium. Lazenby met Whistler, Albert Moore and the Pre-Raphaelites; and was invited to their studios. In the meantime, he was building up the oriental warehouse as the firm's most profitable department. Twelve years after joining the firm he asked for a partnership. When this was refused he determined to open his own shop. His future father-in-law, a Brook Street tailor, lent him £1,500 and backed a loan of a further £1,000 and Liberty leased half a shop in Regent Street, where he was joined by a former Farmer and Rogers employee, a Japanese boy and a sixteen year old girl. He began selling Eastern silks, but was soon importing Japanese porcelain, wallpapers, fans, statuettes and other curios. As his shop prospered so it expanded, eventually moving to its present site.

A little later a costume department was set up 'to establish the craft of dressmaking upon some hygienic, intelligible and progressive basis, uninfluenced by the ateliers of Paris', under the direction of E.W. Godwin, the architect and designer. In 1889 Liberty's opened a clothes and fabrics shop in Paris.

Liberty's began to commission furniture to supplement those pieces they imported from the East, and this was made in the Soho workshops of a Frenchman, Ursin Fortier. In 1883 a Furnishing and Decorative Studio was established, directed by Leonard F. Wyburd. Many of the studio's early designs are either of Eastern inspiration or else within the style of the Aesthetic Movement, then at its height. Since Liberty's was also importing and selling some European, particularly German, furniture, the various designers working for them soon developed their own designs, based on an amalgamation of the English Arts and Crafts designs then being made and the more finished look of Continental furniture.

The imported silks and other textiles were soon supplemented by those made in England, as Liberty's associated itself with various manufacturers. In the late 1880s, Liberty's went one step further, and began to commission original designs for a variety of fabrics, from silks to chintzes, in dress and furnishing weights, from leading designers such as C.F. Annesley Voysey, Lindsay P. Butterfield, Sidney Mawson, J. Scarrett-Rigby and Arthur Silver, founder of the Silver Studio. The fabrics were woven and printed for Liberty's by a variety of outside firms, some of which had close connections with them. Some of these furnishing fabrics were used to upholster or accompany their furniture.

Liberty's began to import Art Nouveau objects from the Continent in the final years of the century. Pewter items by J.P. Kayser & Sohn of Krefeld (Kayserzinn), Walter Scharf & Co. of Nuremberg and L. Lichtinger of Munich encouraged the firm to essay their own metalwork. In late 1898 Arthur Lazenby Liberty commissioned some vessels in silver as well as some silver and gold jewellery, which was first shown in May 1899. The range was given the title of 'Cymric', and the silver was given the hallmark of Ly & Co. Although most of this early silver and jewellery was made by various London manufacturers, Liberty's soon went into a loose association with the Birmingham firm of W.H. Haseler, a manufacturing goldsmiths and jewellers who were to make the bulk of future Cymric wares. The hallmark was changed to L&C in three conjoined diamonds. A new company, Liberty & Co. (Cymric) Ltd. was registered in 1901 to formalize the collaboration between the two firms. A new trademark, L&CC Ltd. in four conjoined circles was registered, but was only rarely used.

The first items of Liberty pewter appeared in November 1901. All of it was manufactured by Haseler, and the generic name of 'Tudric' was given to the range. The individual pieces are found with a variety of marks, such as 'Tudric Pewter by Liberty & Co', 'English Pewter' and 'Solkets', and nearly always accompanied by a design number.

The curious fact which differentiated Liberty's from other shops is that whereas all the others promoted the names and reputations of each of their designers, Liberty's insisted on their complete anonymity. The range of Art Nouveau was extended by Liberty silver and pewter, which used a simplified version of the Celtic entrelac as a decorative motif, often allied with a striking blue and green enamel with occasional touches of red. In combination with plain lines and occasional organic features, it created a new and purely English aspect of Art Nouveau. It would seem that the choice of Celtic decoration was made by A.L. Liberty under the influence of John Llewellyn, who had become a director of Liberty's and was in charge of the new metalwork venture. Some of their designers responded with alacrity, in particular Archibald Knox, a Manxman, and Rex Silver, Arthur Silver's son. Other designers who submitted work to Liberty's included Oliver Baker, Bernard Cuzner, Mr. and Mrs. Arthur Gaskin and Jessie M. King. Certain of these designs are known because they were exhibited at various Arts and Crafts exhibitions, where designers had to be named, or because they were illustrated in contemporary magazines. Other models are attributable by comparison with the designer's known style. But the matter is made more difficult by the destruction of the company's records and their insistence on extending anonymity by frequently changing and adapting designs during the manufacture of items.

The result of such tampering with designs was, as it happened, the emergence of a recognisable 'Liberty style'. This was so well publicised that in Italy Art Nouveau in general is known as 'Stile Liberty'.

It seems at least possible that A.L. Liberty himself, in common with most critics and artists working in England, really had no idea what Art Nouveau was. He was scathing about what he called 'the fantastic motif which it pleases our Continental friends to worship as *l'art nouveau*', while at the same time fostering the creation of Art Nouveau designs in what he apparently believed was a historicist style, and educating the English eye to this style by importing fine Art Nouveau pewter from Germany, Zsolnay pottery from Hungary, and Gouda and other pottery decorated with floral Art Nouveau designs from the Netherlands.

In Britain he encouraged and sold a fine range of art pottery, from Barum Ware to Moorcroft. He also sold 'Clutha' glass designed by Christopher Dresser, George Walton and others, made by James Cooper & Sons of Glasgow, as well as glass made by James Powell & Sons of Whitefriars. A number of Tudric pewter items were made with fitted glass liners in Clutha glass as well as glass from Powell, while a number of Moorcroft bowls and vases were fitted with Tudric pewter bases or feet. Moorcroft reserved certain designs exclusively for Liberty's, as did the Royal Doulton Pottery. Liberty also sold a wide range of Wedgwood, Poole and Ruskin pottery.

The Art Nouveau era for Liberty's lasted till the outbreak of war in 1914. In the post war years furniture was largely confined to imitations of Tudor and Queen Anne designs, while metalware tended towards more simplified designs. Some of the Art Nouveau designs in silver and pewter, however, continued to be manufactured throughout the nineteen twenties.

1

The 'Thebes' stool. This was one of Liberty's earliest and most popular furniture designs. Based loosely on 'an Egyptian model', it consisted of three curved legs set into a curved seat, itself made from a single block of wood. First made in 1884, Liberty's went on making it in oak and mahogany until about 1907. The same name was used for a four-legged low stool slung with a thonged leather seat.

2

The 'Wylye' oak tea table, c.1904. Probably designed by Leonard F. Wyburd, this three-legged table was a variant of the three-legged 'Thebes' stool. The circular top with its upswept edges enabled the table to be used as an indoor plant stand.

3

Mahogany table, each leg decorated with a stylised floral panel in marquetry of various coloured woods. The legs, tiers and stretchers form an intricate design which changes with perspective.

4

Mahogany cradle, swinging freely from firm uprights decorated in marquetry of various coloured woods and inlaid with abalone shell.

5

Mahogany display cabinet, the two glazed doors separated by a central panel decorated with a stylised motif in marquetry of various coloured woods. A similar decorated panel separates the two doors. The motifs are inlaid with mother-of-pearl and abalone shell.

6

Detail of the inlaid marquetry motif in the central panel of the mahogany display cabinet shown in the previous illustration.

7

Fall front desk in mahogany with marquetry of various coloured woods, made in Liberty's workshops, c.1898.

8

Display cabinet in which the traditional shape and design is enlivened by the curved leading on the glazed upper doors and the intricate metalwork of the huge hinges on the lower door.

9

'Nerissa', silk dress and tea jacket in velveteen with gauze front, collar and cuffs, with embroidered design in appliqué. This and the following three illustrations are from a catalogue published in 1905 by Liberty and Co. A great deal of the charm of these illustrations lies in their depiction of Liberty furnishings and accessories including, here, a necklace.

10

'Jacqueline', described in the catalogue as a 'French 15th Century indoor gown. Robe of soft-draping velveteen, silk-crape sash and tucked collar of net with hand-embroidered border.' This model is shown wearing a curious piece of jewellery over her head. There is a Tudric pewter candlestick on the table in the foreground.

11

'Amelia', described as an 'Empire Evening Gown with coat. Robe of Orion satin embroidered in harmonious colouring. Coat of silk-velvet lined with satin; colar, cuffs and belt embroidered with silk and appliqué of velvet.' The model is posed against a screen inlaid in marquetry and with stained glass panels. A Tudric pewter vase stands on a table in the background.

12

'Henrietta', described as a 'Charles II Home Gown. Robe of flowered Tyrian silk, with high-waisted bodice of velveteen. Fichu and sleeve frills in crape.' The illustration also shows curtains and cushion covers in an Art Nouveau fabric.

13

'Peacock feather' fabric, designed by Arthur Silver, founder
of the Silver Studio. It was roller printed on cotton in green
and shades of blue and yellow ochre on a royal blue ground.
Printed for Liberty's by the Rossendale Printing Co., c.1887.

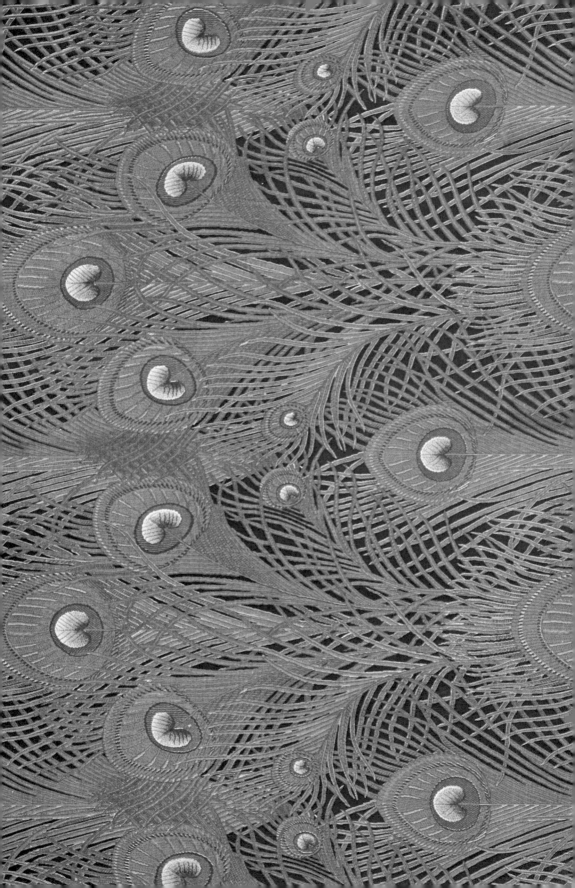

14

Art Nouveau furnishing fabric, designed for Liberty by Harry Napper in 1900. On Arthur Silver's death in 1896, the Silver Studio was run by Napper until Silver's sons were old enough to take over the design studio.

15

Art Nouveau furnishing fabric designed for Liberty by J. Scarrett Rigby in 1897. Rigby was one of Liberty's leading fabric designers.

16

Floral fabric designed by Lindsay P. Butterfield. This was roller printed for Liberty's by G.P. & J. Baker, c.1900.

17

Top row: Three silver and enamel pendants; the one on the left with Celtic entrelacs characteristic of Archibald Knox's designs, the central one showing a simplified interlacing, and the one on the right in an aerial Art Nouveau shape.

2nd row: A gold cloak-clasp set with six pearls. This is an exceptionally free-flowing organic leaf shape reminiscent of the best French or Belgian Art Nouveau designs.

3rd row: Two versions of a brooch designed by Archibald Knox, one in gold and the other in silver, with enamels in warm colours for the gold, cool for the silver.

4th row: Gold and enamel brooch set with three seed pearls and with an amethyst drop.

5th row: Gold and enamel brooch set with mother-of-pearl.

18

Gold necklace set with opals and almandines, probably designed by Archibald Knox, in its original fitted case.

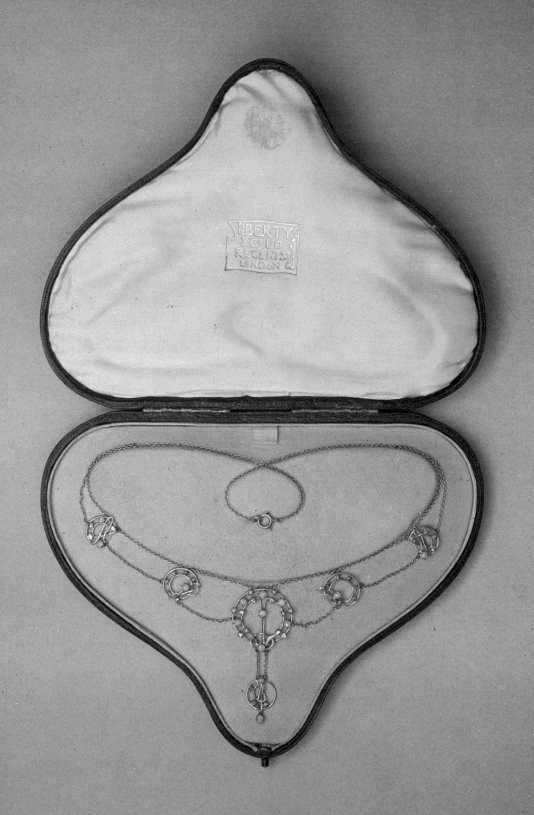

19

Silver and enamel waist or cloak clasps: 1908 (*above*), 1907 (*centre left*), 1910 (*centre right*), 1907 (*below left)* and 1900 (*below right*).

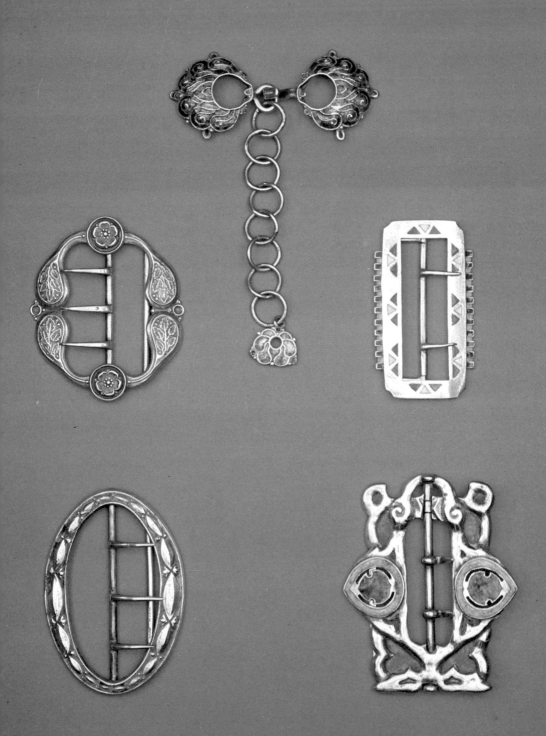

20

Top row: Silver and enamel buckle shaped in the letters ER, designed by Archibald Knox and made in 1910 to commemorate the Coronation of King Edward VII the following year *(left)*. Cymric silver and enamel openwork clasp with a cabochon turquoise, 1901 *(right)*.
2nd row: Cymric silver buckle with Celtic decoration designed by Knox, 1902 *(left)*. Silver and mother-of-pearl buckle with stylised openwork leaves, 1904 *(right)*.
3rd row: Cymric silver and enamel buckle with stylised leaves, designed by Knox, 1902 *(left)*. Silver and enamel buckle with flowing lines, 1900 *(right)*.
4th row: Cymric silver and enamel buckle, 1903 *(left)*. Cymric silver and enamel buckle with Celtic entrelacs, designed by Knox, 1903 *(right)*.

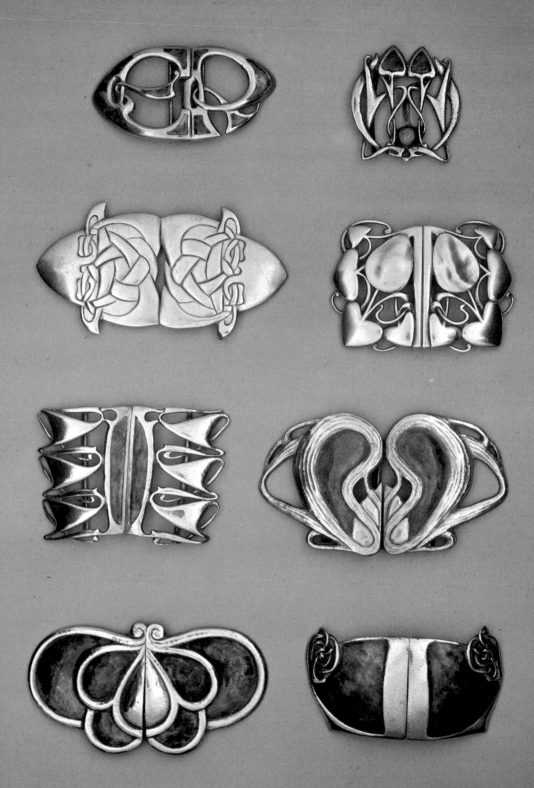

21

Examples of eight different button designs in silver and enamel, 1900 to 1903. Those on the top row, left, also have mother-of-pearl centres. Many different patterns were produced and they were normally sold in boxed sets of six. As with flatware, it is not unusual to find matched sets in which some of the buttons are marked 'L & Co' while others are marked with the Hutton or Haseler marks. It is also common to find them in unmarked boxes, or boxes bearing the names of various provincial retailers.

22

Cymric silver and enamel cigarette case with a Celtic knot decoration on the top face, designed by Archibald Knox.

23

Top row: Silver Celtic pattern waist clasp designed by Rex Silver, 1908 *(left)*. Silver and enamel waist clasp, 1908 *(right)*.
2nd row: Silver and enamel waist clasp, 1912 *(left)*. Waist clasp with flower heads and birds in silver and enamel, designed by Jessie M. King, 1906 *(right)*.
3rd row: Two buckles designed by Oliver Baker; set with a turquoise matrix cabochon, 1903 *(left)*, set with four opals, 1902 *(right)*.
4th row: Silver and enamel waist clasp, 1903 *(left)*. Silver waist clasp with turquoise matrix cabochons, 1901 *(right)*.

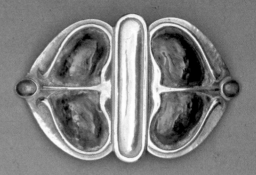

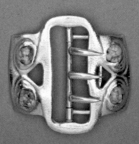

24

Cymric silver clock with mottled blue and green enamelled dial, 1918.

25

Cymric silver carriage clock with a stylised enamel motif in red and green, 1910. The mottled green enamel clock face is marked with the letters for Festina Lente instead of figures. Another frequently used motto replacing the figures on Liberty clocks was Tempus Fugit.

26

Three serving spoons, a knife, a fork and a caddy spoon. The central silver spoon is dated 1899, the other items are silver with enamel. Identical designs are found with the marks of Liberty & Co., W.H. Haseler, G.L. Connell and W. Hutton & Sons. While Haseler and Hutton, who both manufactured items for Liberty, had a fairly small retail business, Connell was a major retailer. The knife in this set forms part of a boxed christening set in which all the matched items are marked 'L & Co' except for the knife which is marked 'G.L.C.'

27

Above: Large matchbox holder in silver with applied enamel motif, 1904.

Below: Two pairs of menu or card holders. The pair above is inscribed with the following mottoes: 'Toute chose au délice conspire/Mettez vous en votre humeur de rire' (All things conspire towards delight/Put yourself in the mood for laughter) and 'On est savant quand on boit bien/Qui ne sait boire ne sait rien' (One is wise when one drinks well/He who knows not how to drink knows nothing), 1902, 1904.

28

Cymric silver hot water jug, 1900. King Edward VII gave Christmas presents of this model some years later.

29

Silver vase of inverted cone shape set on three projecting feet, the body set with three turquoise matrix cabochons. Designed by Archibald Knox, 1905.

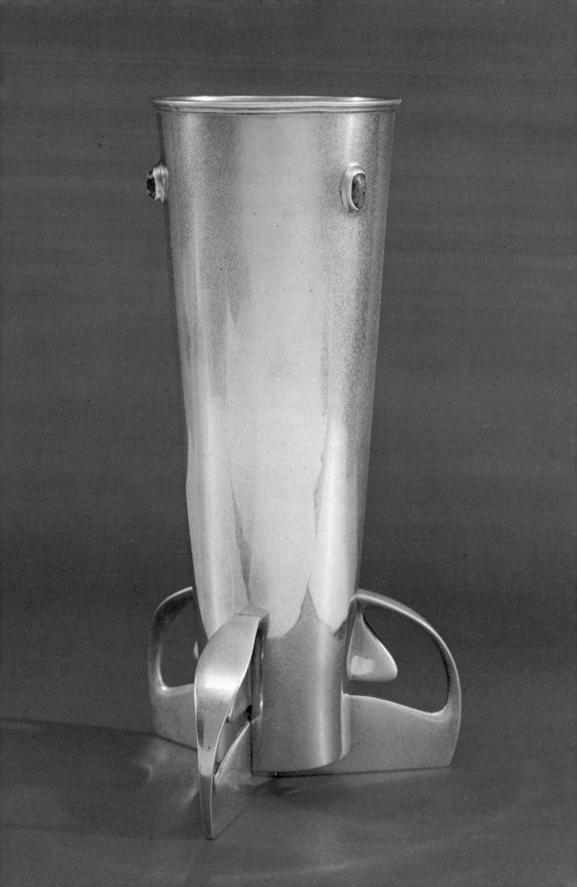

30

Cymric silver candlestick with four enamelled motifs on the base of an elaborate Celtic roundel set in a blue heart, c.1901.

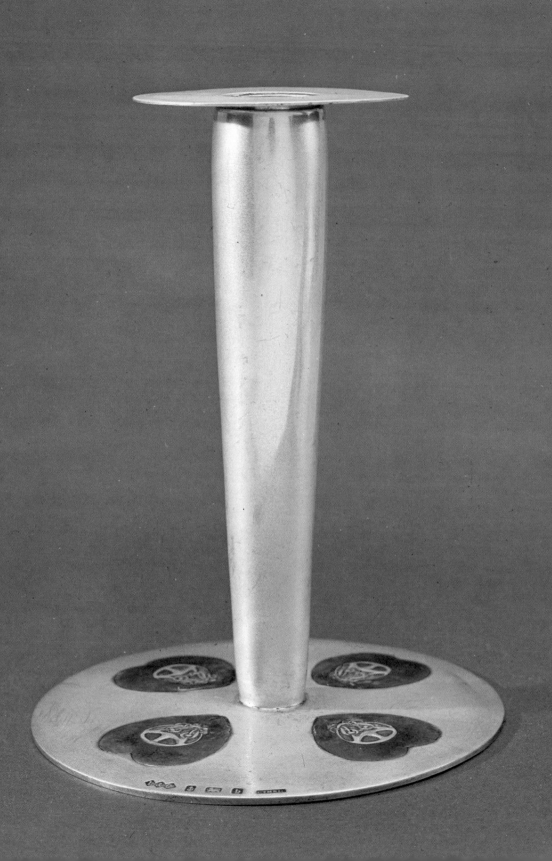

31

Three silver and enamel photograph frames. Each of the models was available in several sizes and often with a choice of rectangular or circular opening. Identical models are found with Liberty, Haseler, Hutton, Connell and Craythorne marks.

32

Cymric silver and enamel spoons. They were sold in matching sets as well as in sample sets of six or twelve different designs in fitted cases. Several models were given design names, including *Medea* (*top row, first left*) and *Sarepta* (*bottom row, second from right*).

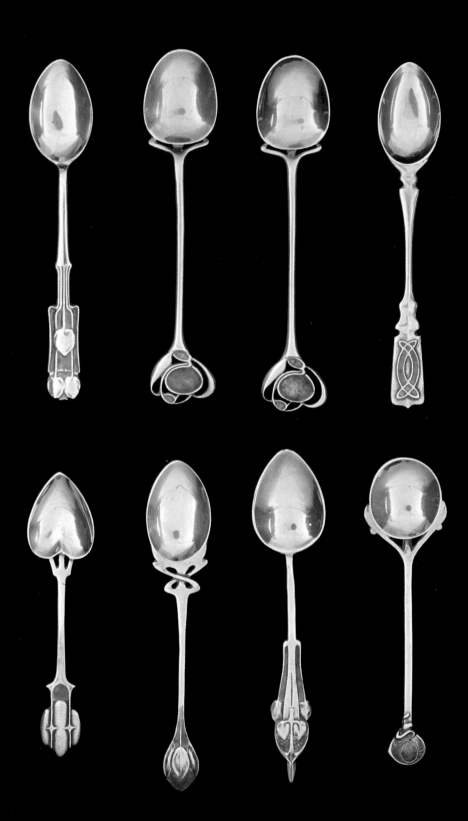

33

Above: Cymric silver and enamel napkin ring with decoration in the form of stylised interlaced plant motifs, 1904.
Below: Stud box in silver and enamel, designed by Archibald Knox, 1907. The inside is padded and lined with silk.

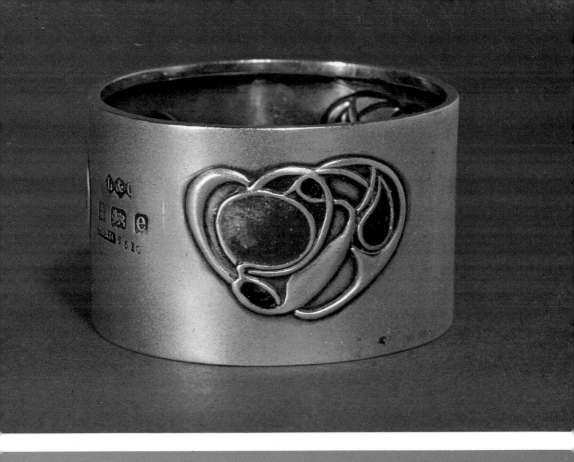

34

Rear: Tudric pewter dish, the rim decorated with five open knot motifs, each set with two pieces of abalone shell. Model No. 0109 C1902.
Front: Tudric pewter jug with cane-covered handle designed by Archibald Knox, c.1904.

35

Tudric pewter floriform vase, the handles treated organically to emerge from the base like plant stems, c.1903.

36

Pewter vase designed by Archibald Knox. The bullet shape, set within three handles which act as a base for the vase, appears like a truncated space rocket. The upper section is decorated with interlaced formalized plant forms.

37

Tudric pewter candlestick with blue enamel studs on the base, designed by Archibald Knox. Variations of this design were produced by Liberty but they were never as successful as the original.

38

Macintyre vase designed by William Moorcroft. The trade name for this range of art pottery, introduced in 1898, was Florian Ware though the elaborately gilt floral style of this vase dates from 1903. Florian ware was sold at Tiffany's in New York, Geo. Rouard in Paris and at Liberty's in London, but the connection with Liberty's strengthened with the growing friendship between Arthur Lasenby Liberty and William Moorcroft. Several designs were made exclusively for Liberty and have a special 'Made for Liberty & Co.' mark. When Moorcroft left Macintyre to set up his own works at Cobridge in 1913, Liberty was closely involved and remained a leading outlet for his wares.

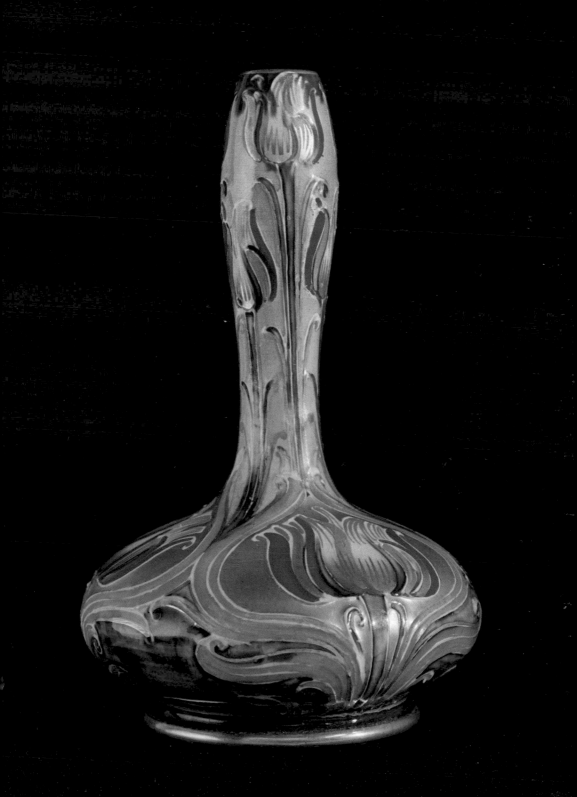

39

Two Moorcroft vases and a square box and cover in the *Red Flamminian* design, registered in 1905. Made at Macintyre in about 1906, these were all marked 'Made for Liberty & Co.' and signed 'W. Moorcroft'. The same models, with the circular roundels outlined in white slip, were also produced in green glazes. Variations occur in some wares where the glaze is slightly streaked with blue, seemingly dripped from the roundel.

40

Moorcroft bowl painted with *Eventide* pattern of orange and green trees among green and yellow hills against a red and orange sky. Set on a stemmed foot of hammered Tudric pewter marked 'Liberty & Co.'

41

Flambé vase by William Moorcroft, painted with a frieze of red trees over an orange ground. Although Moorcroft had attempted this process at Macintyre, it was not until 1919 that he built his own flambé kilns at Cobridge. He experimented there over a number of years to produce a wide variety of effects and colours with varying success. As he was never able to standardise the flambé wares because of the unpredictability of the glaze, each item has a claim to being unique.

42

Two Moorcroft bowls with landscape patterns. *Dawn*, a salt-glaze bowl with blue trees and hills against a pink sky, the outside of the bowl painted with pink, yellow and blue chevrons *(above). Moonlit Blue,* with green trees and hills outlined against a rich dark blue ground. The bowl is set on a wide foot of Tudric hammered pewter, marked 'Liberty & Co.' *(below).*

43

A massive Ruskin vase in high-fired flambé glaze, resting on a high-fired stand. The Ruskin Pottery, named in tribute to the critic John Ruskin, was established in 1899 by William Howson Taylor, son of the head of Birmingham School of Art. Howson Taylor developed a variety of art pottery at his West Smethwick works. The range of rich flambé effects, high-fired to a temperature of 1600 degrees centigrade, produced some of the most beautiful art pottery made. He continued to work until 1935, dying some two months after ceasing production.

44

A pair of Dutch ceramic candlesticks designed by Henri Breetvelt and decorated by Jan Van Schaik. Marked 'Liberty & Co.' Liberty's sold a great deal of Dutch pottery with floral Art Nouveau decoration. A number of models were exclusive to Liberty's in England, and these were sometimes marked with Liberty's name and the initials of designers and decorators, but excluded the manufacturer's name.

45

Above: A Verat Gouda ceramic night light.
Below: A Platelbakkerij Borel candleholder designed by P. Schoonhoven.

46

A tall two-handled Dutch vase made at the Platelbakkerij
Astra at Arnhem.

47

Barum ware vase with dragon handles. Trailed slip and sgraffito decoration of fishes and marine motifs.

48

Group of iridescent glass vessels made at the Johann Loetz
Witwe works in Klostermühle, Bohemia. Liberty's sold much
of this glass, describing it in their 1903 catalogue as 'a new
lustrous glass'. The five miniatures in front were used as scent
bottles, and bear a circular paper label printed 'Liberty & Co.
London' on the base.